Contents

Meet the guinea pigs

Guinea pigs, like this one, make very good pets.

Guinea pigs are animals that come from South America. They are small and furry with large front teeth. Guinea pigs belong to a group of animals called cavies.

Newborn

1 day

1 week

This capybara is the largest kind of cavy.

The largest kind of cavy is the capybara. Wild guinea pigs are brown. In this book, the guinea pigs are brown, white and black.

There are three main types of guinea pig. There are short-haired, long-haired and rough-haired guinea pigs.

5

1 month

8 months

10 months

Newborn

A female guinea pig is called a **sow**. This sow is about to have pups.

This female guinea pig is ready to give birth. A baby guinea pig is called a **pup**. First one tiny pup slides out. It is soon followed by another and then another.

Newborn

1 day

1 week

A group of newborn pups is called a **litter**.

This sow cleans her pup as soon as it is born.

When the pups are first born, they are wet and sticky. The mother licks them clean. The pups can see as soon as they are born. They open their eyes and look around.

1 month   8 months   10 months

First day

This pup is only one day old.

This **pup** has only just been born. She is still wet. Even though she has just been born, she can see and hear well. She is soon running about. She sniffs the hay and starts to explore.

Newborn

1 day

1 week

This pup is having her first drink of milk.

The pup has smelt her mother's milk. She pushes her head under her mother and finds a **teat**. Now the pup is having her first drink of milk.

1 month

8 months

10 months

1 week

This pup nibbles on some grass.

Guinea pig **pups** are timid and keep close to
their mother. This pup has found some grass
to eat. She nibbles the grass with her long
front teeth.

Newborn

1 day

1 week

Loud noises scare pups.

A loud noise scares the pups. They run and hide in the long straw. After a little while, one of the pups pokes his head out to see if it is safe to come out.

1 month

8 months

10 months

1 month

This pup is doing a handstand!

Like all young animals, the guinea pig **pups** like to play. They sniff, rush around and squeak loudly. Running and playing keeps them fit.

Newborn

1 day

1 week

These pups sleep near each other.

Guinea pigs like to be with other guinea pigs. When the pups are tired, they snuggle up together to sleep. The pups know their mother's smell and they know each other's.

1 month

8 months

10 months

2–5 months

This condor is hunting for wild guinea pigs.

Wild guinea pigs must always be on the look out for danger. Large birds, like this **condor**, hunt for wild guinea pigs.

Newborn

1 day

1 week

This guinea pig stands still when he sees the condor.

Guinea pigs have short legs so they cannot run very fast. If there is danger, a guinea pig may stand very still instead of running away. This guinea pig has seen the condor. He stands still so that the condor will not notice him.

1 month

8 months

10 months

8 months

boar

These guinea pigs are ready to start their own families.

At eight months, the guinea pigs are fully grown. They are now ready to start their own families. A large brown male, called a **boar**, joins the group.

Newborn

1 day

1 week

The male guinea pig sniffs the female guinea pig.

The boar growls deeply and creeps around one of the **sows**. The sow sniffs his face and soon they **mate**.

63 days later

This sow likes to eat juicy sweetcorn.

The baby guinea pigs grow inside the **sow** for 63 days, before they are ready to be born. The sow gets very hungry and eats more food.

Newborn

1 day

1 week

The sow pulls away the sticky bag that covers this pup.

After 63 days, the sow gives birth to her **pups**. The sow hides away in the grass to have her pups. She pulls away the sticky bag that covers each one.

1 month

8 months

10 months

1–3 weeks

These pups quickly learn their mother's smell.

The new mother works hard looking after her newborn **pups**. She licks them to keep them clean. The pups soon learn their mother's smell.

Newborn

1 day

1 week

The sow watches over her pups as they play.

The **sow** watches over her pups all the time. The pups play in the straw. When the sow wants her pups to feed she gives a special grunt. The pups hear the special grunt and rush to drink her milk.

1 month

8 months

10 months

3 weeks

The guinea pig pups keep close to their mother.

The young **pups** do not like to be left alone. If their mother walks away from them, they run after her.

Newborn

1 day

1 week

By three weeks, the pups are old enough to join the other guinea pigs.

The young pups grow very quickly. Soon, they are able to join all the other guinea pigs. Many new pups have been born and are growing up.

A sow can produce five **litters** of pups in a year!

1 month   8 months   10 months

This boa snake likes to eat guinea pigs.

24

Wild guinea pigs have many enemies. Large birds, like the **condor**, hunt for guinea pigs. **Pumas** and other animals also hunt for them. Even snakes hunt for wild guinea pigs.

Newborn

1 day

1 week

This guinea pig smells danger.

Guinea pigs have a good sense of smell. This guinea pig is sniffing the air. He can smell a snake nearby and hides in the long grass. The snake does not notice him. Not all the guinea pigs are so lucky.

1 month

8 months

10 months

Living with people

There are many guinea pigs in South America.

Wild guinea pigs come from South America. They live on the grassy **plains** and on the slopes of the Andes mountains. Guinea pigs like to live in groups.

Guinea pigs live in groups called colonies.

These guinea pigs are allowed to run freely in the yard.

These guinea pigs are kept by people who live in the Andes mountains. Guinea pigs kept as pets may live for up to eight years.

Some guinea pigs live much longer than eight years. Snowball, the pet guinea pig, lived for nearly 15 years!

Life cycle

Newborn pup

1 week old

1 month old

8 months old

10 months old

Fact file

A guinea pig's front teeth never stop growing. Pet guinea pigs need to chew carrots or even a piece of wood to stop their teeth becoming too long.

A guinea pig is about 30 centimetres long – as long as a ruler – and weighs about 0.5 kilograms.

A female may have up to four **pups** at the same time, but she has only two **teats**, so the pups have to take turns to feed.

Glossary

boar   male guinea pig

condor   a large bird that lives in the Andes mountains of South America

litter   a group of newborn pups who have the same mother

mate   to come together (a female and a male) to produce young

plains   flat, open countryside

puma   a large, wild cat that lives in the Andes mountains of South America

pup   a young guinea pig from the time it is born until it is old enough to look after itself

sow   female guinea pig

teat   a place from where a baby can drink milk from its mother

Index

32

Life cycle of a
GUINEA PIG

Angela Royston

Heinemann
LIBRARY

First published in Great Britain by Heinemann Library
Halley Court, Jordan Hill, Oxford OX2 8EJ
a division of Reed Educational and Professional Publishing Ltd

Heinemann is a registered trademark of Reed Educational and Professional Publishing Limited.

OXFORD   MELBOURNE   AUCKLAND
IBADAN   JOHANNESBURG   GABORONE
PORTSMOUTH NH   CHICAGO

Designed by Celia Floyd
Illustrations by Alan Fraser
Originated by Dot Gradations, UK
Printed in Hong Kong/China

04 03 02 01 00
10 9 8 7 6 5 4 3 2 1

ISBN 0 431 08405 X

This book is also available in hardback (ISBN 0 431 08400 9).

British Library Cataloguing in Publication Data

Royston, Angela
   Life cycle of a guinea pig. – (Take-off!)
   1.Guinea pigs - Life cycles – Juvenile literature
   I.Title II.Guinea pig
   599.3'592

Acknowledgements
The Publisher would like to thank the following for permission to reproduce photographs:
Bruce Coleman Ltd/Dr Eckart Potts p4; Lanceau/Cogis pp5, 25; Leibenswerte Neerschweinchen, Elrig Hansen c 1998 Kinder Buchverlag Luzern (Sauerlander AG) pp6–9, 11–13, 16, 17, 19–22; NHPA/Daniel Heuclin p24; NHPA/Jany Sauvanet p26; NHPA/Kevin Schafer p14; OSF/W Layer p18; South American Pictures/Tony Morrison p27 Testu/Cogis p15; Vidal/Cogis p23.
Cover photograph: Bruce Coleman
Our thanks to Sue Graves and Stephanie Byars for their advice and expertise in the preparation of this book.

For more information about Heinemann Library books, or to order, please telephone +44(0)1865 888066, or send a fax to +44(0)1865 314091. You can visit our website at www.heinemann.co.uk

Any words appearing in bold, **like this**, are explained in the Glossary.